A Very Young Actress

Written and Photographed by

Jill Krementz

Alfred A. Knopf, New York, 1991

This Is a Borzoi Book
Published by Alfred A. Knopf, Inc.

Copyright © 1991 by Jill Krementz
All rights reserved under International and
Pan-American Copyright Conventions.
Published in the United States by Alfred A. Knopf, Inc.,
New York, and simultaneously in Canada by
Random House of Canada Limited, Toronto.
Distributed by Random House, Inc., New York.

Library of Congress Cataloging-in-Publication Data
Krementz, Jill.
    A very young actress/written and photographed by Jill Krementz.—1st ed.
    p. cm.
    Summary: A ten-year-old girl who starred in a workshop production of *Annie 2*
describes her experiences on- and offstage, from auditions through rehearsals to
opening night.
    ISBN 0-679-40637-9
    1. Acting—Juvenile literature.   2. Gaffney, Lauren—Juvenile literature.
    [1. Acting.   2. Gaffney, Lauren.]   I. Title.
    PN2061.K68   1991
    791'.028'023—dc20   91-52804
                            CIP
                            AC
Manufactured in the United States of America
First Edition

A Very Young Actress

Also by Jill Krementz

The Face of South Vietnam
(with text by Dean Brelis)

Sweet Pea—A Black Girl Growing Up in the Rural South

Words and Their Masters
(with text by Israel Shenker)

The Writer's Image

A Very Young Dancer

A Very Young Rider

A Very Young Gymnast

A Very Young Circus Flyer

A Very Young Skater

A Very Young Skier

A Very Young Musician

The Fun of Cooking

Lily Goes to the Playground

Jack Goes to the Beach

Taryn Goes to the Dentist

Benjy Goes to a Restaurant

Katherine Goes to Nursery School

Jamie Goes on an Airplane

Zachary Goes to the Zoo

Holly's Farm Animals

A Visit to Washington, D.C.

How It Feels When a Parent Dies

How It Feels to Be Adopted

How It Feels When Parents Divorce

How It Feels to Fight for Your Life

All photographs by Jill Krementz
except for page 4, top, and page 15,
top, by Donna Gaffney and page 4,
bottom, by Martha Swope

A Very Young Actress

When I grow up, I definitely want to be an actress. I love being on the stage! My name is Lauren Gaffney, and I'm ten years old. I made my debut just before my eighth birthday in a community production of *Hello Dolly.* I was one of the children singing in the chorus. Since then I've been in *Jesus Christ Superstar, Anything Goes, Showboat,* and *The Sound of Music.*

I have a huge collection of souvenirs from all of my shows—for example, I wore four different hats in *Showboat,* and I saved them all. I even kept the jar of plum jelly which was a prop in the opening scene. It's fun to have the other actors autograph the show cards before I frame them and hang them on my bedroom walls. The best part of being in the theater is making so many new friends.

When I was in *Showboat*, I played the part of Kim, the daughter of Gaylord Ravenal, who was played by Richard White. Since I always play the part of a kid, I now have a huge collection of stage fathers and mothers.

I even have a stage stepmother. In *The Sound of Music* Debby Boone was my governess for the first act, but then she married my "dad," Captain Von Trapp. I played the part of Marta, the second youngest in the family.

Of course I love recess. We have a huge tire playground which is so much fun.

In my real family I *am* the youngest. I live with my parents and brothers, Ryan and Brendan, in New Jersey. My pet rabbit is named Thumper, and my two best friends are Robyn and Katherine.

When I'm not acting, I go to school like other kids. I'm in the fourth grade, and my teacher's name is Mrs. Cash. My favorite subjects are math and English.

I'm a member of Girl Scout Troop #362. We meet on Monday afternoons after school and have lots of activities such as making crafts, learning songs, and going on overnight camp-outs. I earned eight badges this year and sold seventy-five boxes of Girl Scout Cookies. My mom still has a box in the bottom of her closet.

On Wednesday afternoons I have a voice lesson with Gene McLaughlin in New York City. I wear an elastic support around my waist which reminds me to push out with my abdomen when I'm singing. This helps with breath control and projection, which are important for singing on the stage.

Sometimes Gene shows me a picture of a face when he's explaining how to position my mouth and get the best sound from my vocal cords.

On Thursdays Mom drives me to the city again for a dance lesson with Charles Hughes. He coaches and trains a lot of the top performers.

We start our lesson at the barre so I can warm up my muscles. Then I put on my tap shoes. We work on my technique and new routines. I love the names of the different steps. There's a "flap" and a "slap" and a "scuffle" and a "shuffle." A "flap ball change" is a combination of two steps—a "flap" and a "ball change." A "flap" is when you tap the front part of your foot on the floor, and a "ball change" is changing your weight from the ball of one foot to the other.

Sometimes I have to be reminded to keep my arms in the proper position.

One of the most important people in my professional life is my agent, Ayn Lauren. She's been representing me for about a year. Besides sending me on auditions, she gives me advice about my career. For example, she helps us choose a photographer for my "headshots," which have to be updated about once a year. My résumé gets stapled on the back of each photo, and it has to be updated with every job I do. It lists all my stage, television, and film experience as well as my vital statistics: height, weight, dress size, and social security number. I list my date of birth as well as my "age range," which is seven to eleven.

In order to get a part, you have to audition for directors and casting people. Some auditions are "closed," which means you have to be sent by your agent. Others are "open," which means anyone can try out for the role.

Last year there was an "open call" for the role of Annie in a new musical called *Annie 2*. There were so many of us that we waited outside the theater for hours. They gave us buttons and fans.

Lots of girls were "cut," but I got a "call back." On my call back I got cut, but five months later I auditioned again for the workshop production of *Annie 2* in Connecticut. This time I got the job! I got picked to play the role of Annie!

Since I was going to have to move to Connecticut for rehearsals and the run of the show, my mom and I had to talk to the principal of my school. We went over my schedule so I could keep up with my schoolwork while I was away. On my last day of school I painted a picture of Annie in art class for my classmates. Then Mom and I packed everything I owned!

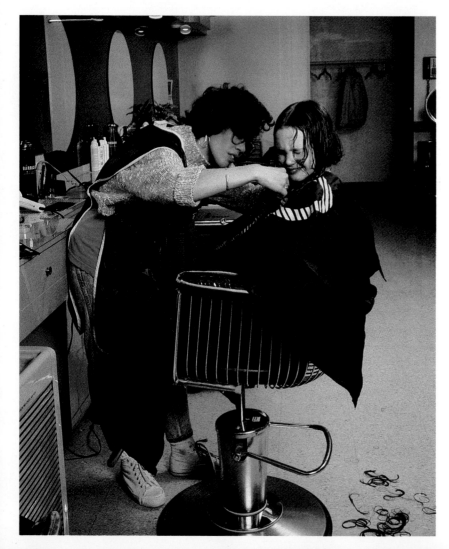

The day before I left, I had to get my hair cut and colored because, as you know, Annie has red hair.

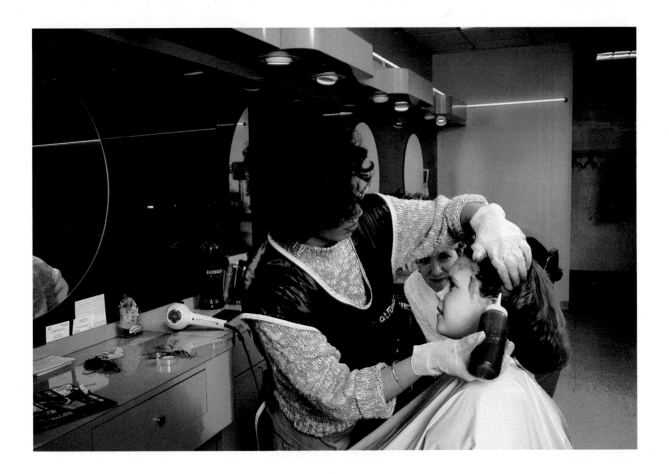

While I was waiting to turn into a redhead, I chatted with my friend Lily, who happened to be getting her bangs cut. She thought I looked pretty weird, but she promised she'd try to come and see the show.

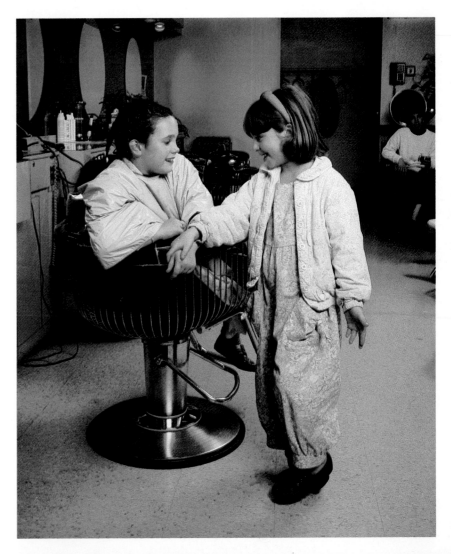

Two hours later when it was all over, my brothers dropped by for a final inspection. They said they hardly recognized me.

I hardly recognized myself! I felt like a new woman.

The entire cast and crew stayed at an inn fifteen minutes from the theater. We were in a village called Ivoryton, which got its name because there used to be a piano-key factory in the village, and ivory had come in by the ton.

The ballroom of our hotel became our classroom every morning from nine to eleven. That was when we did schoolwork with our two tutors. There were five other kids in the show who played orphans—Moriah, Jennifer, Natalia, Blaze, and Lisa.

We were in rehearsal for three weeks. Every morning after "school," Mom drove me to the rehearsal studio. I used the car ride to the studio for my warm-up time. I have a tape recorder with tapes of my piano music which I use for practicing my scales. When you're a singer, it's important to exercise your vocal cords so you don't strain them when you sing.

The entire cast and crew stayed at an inn fifteen minutes from the theater. We were in a village called Ivoryton, which got its name because there used to be a piano-key factory in the village, and ivory had come in by the ton.

The ballroom of our hotel became our classroom every morning from nine to eleven. That was when we did schoolwork with our two tutors. There were five other kids in the show who played orphans—Moriah, Jennifer, Natalia, Blaze, and Lisa.

We were in rehearsal for three weeks. Every morning after "school," Mom drove me to the rehearsal studio. I used the car ride to the studio for my warm-up time. I have a tape recorder with tapes of my piano music which I use for practicing my scales. When you're a singer, it's important to exercise your vocal cords so you don't strain them when you sing.

As soon as I got to the studio, I would go over any script changes with Julie Tucker, the production assistant. While you're still learning your part, you can rehearse with your script. It's called "being on book."

Tom Meehan is the person who wrote the story, and he's also the one who changed my lines every day.

Lots of my scenes were with Harve Presnell, who played the role of Daddy Warbucks.

They put pieces of tape on the floor so you know where to stand. This is called "spiking the stage."

The standing up part was easy. What was harder was when I had to sit on his shoulder and sing!

The director, Martin Charnin, and the choreographer, Peter Gennaro, told us how to say our lines and how to move our bodies on the stage.

Harve and I had a big song together called "When You Smile." Martin told me to concentrate on the words and what they mean whenever I sing a song or speak a line of dialogue.

Whenever I wasn't in a scene with other actors, I practiced my songs with Steven Alper, the musical director. Sometimes I tried singing the songs in different keys until we found the one that sounded best. When we got it right, Steve would say, "Take it from the top," and I would start the song from the beginning.

At the end of every day, I practiced with Chelsea, who plays the role of Sandy. Bill Berloni, Chelsea's trainer, taught me cues and hand signals. I kept some doggie biscuits in my hip pack.

The company rehearsed eight hours a day for three weeks.

Each night after dinner and a few games of Spit with Jennifer, my mom
and I went over lines. Chelsea often came for sleepovers so we could get
to be better friends.

The costume coordinator makes sure that everyone is in the right costume and that they fit. It was very important that I could move around easily while doing all my dance numbers. There was a little plastic-lined pocket sewn in just above my left sleeve cuff to hold treats for Chelsea.

I had to be fitted for a wig even though it hadn't been decided whether or not I would wear one in the show. James Post pinned up my real hair and covered it with a "wig cap," which looks like a stocking. Then he measured my head to be sure the wig would be the right size. If your wig's too small, it can give you a big headache. And if it's too big, it could fall off!

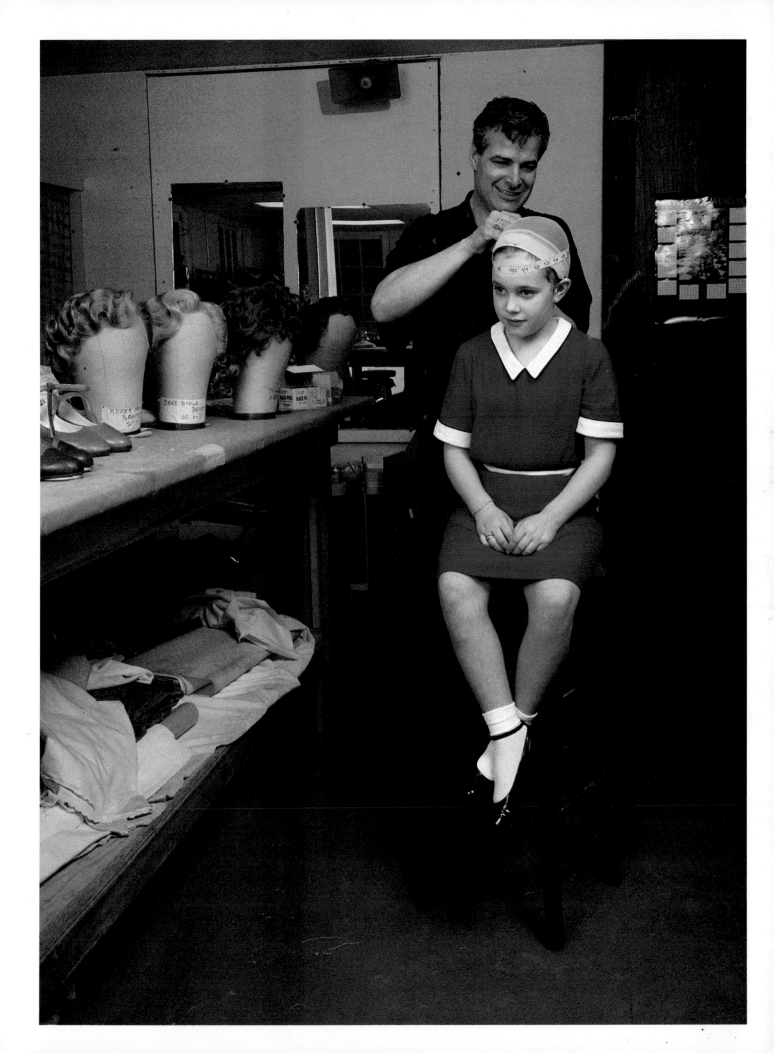

The week before the show opened we moved to the theater for rehearsals on the stage. I shared a dressing room with Jennifer and Natalia.

There was a big chart backstage on the wall which listed all our scenes and costume changes. I wore a white nightie in Scene One, and after that it was my red Annie dress for the whole show.

Working on a stage feels a lot different from working in a small studio. We had four days of technical rehearsals, which means learning to work with costumes, lighting, props, and sets.

There's a big production number called "All Dolled Up" which includes the entire company. Everyone sings and dances. Some of the actors practiced with their costumes, and some didn't.

The theater had to get ready for opening night too. Our pictures and
"bios" were put up in the lobby. And a larger-than-life Annie was hoisted
on top of the theater roof.

Opening night is always exciting. Lots of my relatives sent flowers, and my dad, Brendan, and Ryan drove up from New Jersey.

I sent cards to the cast members telling them to "Break a leg!" which is how people in the theater wish each other good luck.

Thirty minutes before the show begins, the stage manager calls "half hour." After that, no one but the actors can be backstage. Mom gave me a big hug and told me to have a great show.

Putting on my makeup is a good time to "get into character." By that I mean I think about what kind of person Annie is. For the next two hours, I will be Annie Warbucks and not Lauren Gaffney.

Martin came backstage to give us some last minute "notes." It's like the pep talk a coach gives the team before the big game.

He told us not to panic. He said we should go out there and have a good time!

The lights came up and the show began. I hardly recognized Sarah Knapp in her Grace Farrell wig.

When I got to the second scene, where Harve and I sang "When You Smile," even though there was an audience, I wasn't nervous.

The Stark sisters are always trying to ruin my life—on stage, that is. In the show they're called "comic villains."

Lisa sang her solo upside down and everyone clapped. If you think it's easy to belt out a song in that position, try it!

Up until the last scene, everyone did a perfect job.

Then suddenly Chelsea got stage fright. I could hardly get her onstage.

As Annie would say, "Leapin' lizards." Before I knew it, the first performance was over and the audience was clapping . . . and clapping . . . and clapping.

At the party afterwards Martin gave me a big hug.

Annie 2 ran in Connecticut for eight weeks, and you can bet your bottom dollar I loved every minute of it. I learned a lot, made some wonderful new friends, and had a great time. You know what they say—there's no business like show business!

A Note About the Author

Jill Krementz works as a journalist, photographer, and portraitist whose pictures appear regularly in the *New York Times, New York, People, Newsweek,* and many other major periodicals. She has written and photographed more than two dozen books for young readers and adults, including *A Very Young Skier, A Very Young Dancer, A Very Young Rider, A Very Young Gymnast, A Very Young Circus Flyer,* and *A Very Young Skater.* She has also won acclaim for the How It Feels series, dealing with the death of a parent, adoption, divorce, and chronic illness.

Ms. Krementz received the 1984 *Washington Post*/Children's Book Guild Non-fiction Award for "creatively produced books, works that make a difference." She lives in New York City.

A Note on the Type

The text of this book was set in Simoncini Garamond, a modern version by Francesco Simoncini of the type attributed to the famous Parisian type cutter Claude Garamond (ca. 1490–1561). Garamond was a pupil of Geoffroy Tory and is believed to have based his letters on the Venetian models, although he introduced a number of important differences, and it is to him we owe the letter that we know as old-style. He gave to his letters a certain elegance and a feeling of movement that won for their creator an immediate reputation and the patronage of Francis I of France.

Composed by The Sarabande Press, New York, New York; printed and bound by The Kingsport Press, Inc., Kingsport, Tennessee.